Soulful Sweetness

Spiritual nourishment through sacred

poetry

Kayla Rodriguez

His love does not start with your success

Nor does it end when you feel as though you have failed

His love does not begin with your attempts to be righteous

Nor does it cease when you seem to have lost your way

In all circumstances, His love remains

It will wash away every feeling of inadequacy

For it was never meant to be earned

But poured out and received

Don't take the failure to fill the void as a reason to stop searching

Don't take it as confirmation that nothing will be enough

Take it as your sign that your soul is called to something greater

To Someone greater

Don't seek to distract your soul from its cry for more

For it is a cry that shouldn't be ignored

Maybe if you sat in the silence for just a moment longer,

You would hear the cry of your soul

Maybe if you sit in the silence for just a moment longer,

You will begin to hear His call

For every moment of failure to fulfill one's self is a reminder to come home to Jesus.

Every moment of palpable emptiness serves as a reminder that He is the only thing that will satisfy.

Your soul's cry is a response to the absence of the One who formed it

So when you're sitting there in the silence

Let your soul cry louder than it ever has to Him;

Lord,

> *Let the emptiness of my heart*
>
> *Lead me to the fullness of Yours*
>
> *Let the inadequacy of this life*
>
> *Point me to You*
>
> *And lead me to the abundance of life that You have for me*
>
> *Let this dry land*
>
> *Point me to the green pasture that You walk through*
>
> *For the place in which You dwell*

Is the place I desire to be also

I long to be led, Lord

Lead me from this dry land

Into the green pasture

Your one lost sheep wants to come home

Your lost sheep wants to be found

Even if you know Him not,

He knows you by name

He will answer your cry with no hesitation or delay

For He has always been calling you home to Him

The Good Shepherd wastes no time

Running to the 1 sheep, He left the 99 for

Life will feel meaningless until you give it to the One who created it.

How can we appreciate the view from the mountains,

if we do not first go through the valleys?

Don't give shame a place in your heart

Where His grace is supposed to reign

The emptiness we feel without Him

Is the space that is reserved for the fullness of His love

I am most myself when I am closest to You

When I dwell in You, I am most like who I was made to be

When I dwell in my Creator, I have rest

When I dwell in my Creator, each day, I become more and more like the beautiful creation He made me to be

As He continues to refine me

As His love as deep as the ocean shapes and forms me just as the ocean erodes and shapes the rocks of the earth.

I stand in awe of Him

I stand in His presence, in awe of who He is making me to be

In awe of who I always was without even knowing it

I stand in awe as I watch myself change before my very eyes

And contemplate on how I never thought I could be such a beautiful creation

How I never thought I would see myself as a beautiful being

But glory be to God

For He has opened my eyes, and I have seen the beauty that He has made in me.

The beauty that is in me because of the work of His mighty hands

Those who have come to know the heart of God know that there is no condemnation in it

There is no condemnation in a grace so pure

Those who know Him know that He is not a God of condemnation

So do not let your heart condemn you

Let your heart be a reflection of His

One that grants yourself the same grace He continuously grants you

The darkness becomes but a shadow in His light

Just something that is behind us, that is in our past

As we look forward, we see that we are covered by His light and not consumed by darkness

We have taken off the old self and are now a new creation in Christ

Life will always flow from His hands.

Just as the birth of creation began with Him, so does
the re-birth of creation begin with Him

Beauty will always flow from His hands

All beautiful things flow from Him like a river

A river of living water

Through Him, we are reborn into who we were
always born to be

Lord,

There is not one part of my life that I want You to be absent from

I prepare a place for You in my heart

A place that You deserve to inhabit

And in exchange, You prepare a place for me at Your table

A place that could not be earned

A place that I have been gifted through Your blood

There is no bitterness in a grace so sweet

No strings attached, He loves you

He will go out and seek for you just to bring you into
His presence

Time and time again

Lord,

Let the words that are written on Your heart,

Also, be written on mine

The same love that drove Him to the cross is the same love that pursues you now.

I sought life outside of the Lord and came back
empty-handed

I then came to Him, empty-handed, with nothing to
offer, and He looked at me

I kept my head down in shame, feeling the dread of
the rejection wash over me like a wave

This was a familiar feeling

Showing up, giving all I had, leaving with nothing
but empty hands and an empty heart seeking out love
and acceptance

You can imagine my surprise when I felt His hand lift
my head and I could see His beautiful smile.

This was an unfamiliar feeling

A feeling of safety and comfort

Though the feeling was unfamiliar, He was familiar

Somehow, I knew Him

The wave of dread disappeared, and His warm love washed over me

Wave after wave, I became consumed by it

I looked at Him in awe and wonder as He wrapped me in His tender and protective embrace.

As our hearts aligned, I could feel Him speak to me, "You are all I've ever wanted."

So, in my empty hands, I placed my heart and gave it to Him

I sought life outside of the Lord and came back empty-handed

I could offer Him nothing, and He gave me everything

Nothing can separate us from the fullness of His love.

Give Him your burdens, and don't take them back

The more you take the burden upon yourself

The heavier it gets

Leave your burdens where they belong

On the cross where your Savior hung

Where He took on the weight of the whole world.

So you wouldn't have to feel as if you were carrying it
on your shoulders

His first question was not "What have you done?" but

"Where are you?"

His heart has always been after *you*.

Genesis 3:9

There is not one drop of shame in the ocean of love
that He is

There is not one ounce of condemnation in a love so
compassionate

In a God so merciful

In a grace so abundant

Lord,

I want it no other way but Yours

Darkness has no place in the space that He inhabits

The place in which He dwells, darkness will flee from

Allow Him to make His dwelling place within your heart

And watch how the darkness flees with the arrival of His presence

He makes the brightest days out of the darkest nights.

What power do your words have over the words of God?

The Words that spoke light into existence

With four words from His mouth, all darkness ceased to be

The same mouth that spoke the world into being says that you are more precious than all other creation

He says the most beautiful things about you

He who formed you inside of your mother's womb

Who knit you together perfectly

From head to toe, you are His most beautiful creation

You are the only creation that was made in His image

In His perfect image

While you harshly pick out things about yourself that are unsatisfactory to you, that don't meet your expectations,

He reflects on how His hands gently put you together

As you place your hands on your biggest insecurities,

on the parts of yourself that you wish to hide, the

Lord mourns as He is proud of what He has created

The Lord mourns as His most precious creation

wishes to recreate themselves.

Be loved by Jesus,

Love Jesus,

And love like Jesus

We love because He first loved us

1 John 4:19

God wants you to experience Him in all of His fullness.

"You are far more than your struggle."

Says the Lord

"For I did not shame you out of the grave but called

you out of it"

God does not make mistakes.

Therefore a mistake, you are not

Where is the strength in a heart of stone?

A heart that is hardened

That does not allow itself to feel

To hurt

To love

Unlike the heart of stone, the heart of flesh endures it
all

It hurts

It loves

It feels

And yet

After it all

If that heart of flesh remains and does not turn to
stone

It is far stronger than a heart of stone will ever be

You humanize yourself when you admit that you are struggling

You dehumanize yourself when you claim that your struggle is all that you are

You could tell Jesus anything

And He would never think less of you.

It's okay to say, "I didn't deserve that."

Real love does not come from pretending that someone didn't wrong you

It comes from acknowledging that they did and loving them anyway

Getting better is a process.

Be patient with yourself.

Oh, what a blessing it is to be in Your presence

To step into the sweetness of Your love

To live under the covering of Your grace

There will be a day when you say

"I can't wait to wake up tomorrow."

Every person I meet

Is a person I was meant to love

Don't live under the illusion that the things that rip

you apart are the things that make you whole.

Live under the truth that Jesus is the only thing that

will complete you.

In His love, there is fullness.

Apart from His love, we will be met with nothing but emptiness

He left the grave behind Him

So that we may also experience the freedom of

leaving the grave behind us

You are not unreachable.

For the Good Shepherd who leaves the ninety-nine

To find the one,

You are not unreachable

You are not too deep in the valley

To be brought back home

To be carried to the mountains,

You are not too deep in the valley

You are not too broken

For the Great Potter who restores all

Who mends all wounds and holds all things together,

You are not too broken

You are not too lost

To be found

By the One who already sees you

By the One who knows you not by what you have
done,

But by who He made you to be

By who He knows you to be

You are not too lost

In a fallen world

What a blessing it is

To serve a God that is high above all

That is greater than all things

Greater than all doubt and worry

Greater than all fear and despair

His words greater than all the thoughts that cloud our
minds

His love greater than our faults

His grace so boundless that no iniquity is beyond its
reach

His blood so pure that it washes us of all impurity

His embrace so wide that He could fit the entire
world in His arms

If only we would accept His invitation

Into a life greater than the one we are currently living

True life in a fallen world

Oh, what a gift

To know that there is more than what meets the eye

To know that there is hope

To know that there is a Light

In a fallen world

The world is formless and void of meaning

This is the thought that haunts us each day

As we search for a reason

Not realizing that our eyes are closed

And that the reason we are seeking

Is standing there,

Right in front of us

With His arms wide open

For the world is formless and void of meaning

Until He brings meaning to it

Until His presence rushes in

And rescues us

And shows us the truth

Just because the world is dark and void doesn't mean
    that you have to be

You certainly weren't made to be

It can be convincing at times

That all you will ever be is a reflection of this world

You were made to be a reflection of Him

A light in a world that needs it

To think that you are only made for this world's
limits is a deception in itself.

Your Creator is in heaven

Your potential is limitless with He who does the
impossible

You were made for more

Lord,

Help me not to run away from You when I
need You most

Help me not to cling to the chains that You
desire to set me free from

But to cling to You as my soul cries out for rest

Help me to not find comfort in the things that
You gave Your life to deliver me from

Help me to walk in freedom as You have called
me to do

To never label myself by anything other than
who You have said I am

To label myself by the name that You used
when You called me out of the grave

The name that You called me as I stepped from
death into life

Help me to live under the truth that I am free

I am free indeed

Why do you refuse life?

Why do you turn away and refuse to come to Him?

You trust in the things that destroy you

You wrap yourself in them as though they are your
safety blanket

You put your trust in the very things that are ripping
you apart from the inside out

And yet distrust the One who will repair you from
the inside out

You give power to the things that are powerless

You give them power over you and let yourself
become a slave though you were meant to be
free

Only in His presence will it be revealed to you how

powerless your safety blanket of lies are

In His presence, nothing else compares

Under His care, there is freedom

Under His care, there is joy

In His presence, there is no burden that cannot be
lifted

No chain that can't be broken

No heart that can't be healed

No slave that can't be freed

Allow Him to remove your safety blanket of lies

And you will see that true safety is found in His
embrace

As you make Jesus core to who you are

Love will begin to naturally flow out of you

Love will flow out of your heart and will pour into
the hearts of others

Love will pour out into the world around you

A world filled with precious people

Precious people who feel as if they can only dream of
a love so deep and unconditional

Let Jesus be core to who you are

And love will flow out of you like a river

Into a world that is as dry as the desert

People often say,

"There is no room for mistakes."

But I happen to think that the space between human

and immortal

Between imperfection and perfection

Is the space where mistakes happen

And where His grace reigns

There is room for grace

Where your ability cannot reach

His grace covers all

Be the good you don't see in the world

Be the good you wish existed

Leave your shame with the grave.

For where the old life dies,

Shame should die also

Let go of the baggage that is holding you down

And embrace the truth of the Lord

Where grace marks the beginning of new life

I pray that when my heart bleeds at the hands of others,

That all that would flow out is the unconditional love of the Lord

I pray in the moments where my heart is tempted to be drained of all good,

In the moments where it is tempted to be left with nothing but bitterness,

That it would be filled with an abundance of love to give

A heart of flesh is bound to bleed

But what a beautiful flow it is

Oh, to love with a hurting heart

Is to love like Jesus does

Though there are still battles to be fought,

The Lord has already won the war

The One who has already won the war in His power,

Has also the power to win the battle you're facing

Don't give the enemy, the one who has already lost
the war,

The satisfaction of believing that he has the power to
win a battle

For your battle is the Lord's battle

And that is a battle that is bound to be victorious

People are worth loving.

The birds' songs become sweeter when you know He is the One who gives them the song.

The leaves become greener when you know He is the One that gives them color.

The sun shines the brightest when you know that He spoke light into existence.

Nothing can compare to the beauty of creation when you realize that all of it sings His praises.

Praise God

For He has opened my blind eyes

And has shown me the beauty of it all

All of creation has a song of praise to sing to Him

May I never allow my heart to get hardened

And withhold love from the people around me who need it

May the damage that others have caused

Never be the reason that I call myself damaged

I may be imperfect

And hurt

But I am created to love

May I never stop loving

May the hurt never prevent me from doing what I was created to do

May it never prevent me from being who I was made to be

A being of love to give

I will not label myself off of the things that have happened to me

I am not my hurts

I am not my past

May I have a heart that is open to goodness

For a heart that is open to let goodness in is also a heart capable of being filled with goodness to give

Let this love flow out of my heart like a river that never runs dry.

Even when it is not at the surface

Though I have convinced myself that I've pushed it

all the way to the back of my mind,

Somewhere hidden in the dark where it cannot be

found,

The truth is that it lingers above

And is prone to drop at any moment

I am pulled down to the ground in anguish

My heart has dropped into my stomach

I feel so empty yet so heavy

I can barely stand

My heart is heavy

My mind is burdened

I know that the only way for the heaviness to be lifted

Is not by burying it deep underneath,

But by allowing it to come to the surface

Not by pushing it to the back in a desperate attempt to keep it hidden and forgotten

But by bringing it before You

And allowing You to lift the load that I can carry no longer

Lord,

Help me to lay down the burdens that I wish to forget

I know that they are not meant to stay hidden

But brought to the light for healing to take place

In Your presence alone, Lord, is where that is possible

So I ask You to give me the strength to bring this heaviness before You

And to lay it at Your feet where it belongs instead of carrying it on my shoulders

Heaviness is meant to be lightened.

Burdens are meant to be lifted.

Rest is made for the weary

Who carry the weight that was never meant for their shoulders

For He carried it all

And defeated it all

It is all possible in His presence

Come to me, all you who are weary and burdened, and I will give you rest.

Matthew 11:28-30

Who would I be without love?

I embrace the image I was made in

Because I was made in the image of Love Himself,

I refuse to be an empty shell of a human

Be intentional with your kindness and generous with your love

The smallest details often mean the world

And the smallest of moments are often the sweetest

Imagine the joy of the blind

When the first thing they saw when they were finally healed,

Was the sweet smile of their Healer

Their first gaze when their eyes were finally opened

Was upon the Man who opened them

Oh, what a blessing to be able to say

That the first thing you saw was the face of the Son of God

To say that you stared beauty in His eyes

And were forever changed

Oh, what a blessing to be able to say

That the first thing you saw was the very face of Light

After seeing nothing but darkness for your whole life

Let my every breath

Praise the Lord

Be proud of the little accomplishments

And celebrate all of the milestones.

No matter how small you think they may be

Your struggles do not make you less worthy of love.

I can finally say

That I don't miss the places

That caused me the most damage

Where He sends you,

Where His presence leads you,

His presence will also be

There is beauty in the sadness

That doesn't sting as much as it used to

There is beauty in the sadness

That shows you that you are getting better

The things that take the most time

Are often the things that are most meaningful

Beautiful things take time

But they are always worth the wait

I am filled with love to give

And kindness to show

I refuse to be shallow

Only because I'm afraid of drowning

I am meant to love and care deeply

I know the One who walks on the water will sustain

me

Lord,

I want people to be as precious in my sight as they are in Yours

More valuable than rubies

And worth more than gold

The Lord is generous with His love

My heart is not only full

But it overflows

Patience is not just waiting

But being content in the waiting

There is nothing

His love can't cover

Praise God

For all of the little victories,

Praise God

How beautiful it is

To know that you are not defined by what you do

That you are not your good deeds

Or your bad

That your actions do not determine your worth

Good or bad

That there is nothing that can make you more or less loved,

Nothing that can make you more or less valuable

Your worth is in Him alone

And to Him,

You are worth His life

The beauty of His presence is that it is everywhere

The beauty is that He not only meets you where you are,

But that there is no distance that He won't travel to come and find you

Right there in your room,

Can become the secret place

In the intimacy of sweet solitude with Jesus,

Is where the relationship can start

Make room for love in your heart

So that bitterness has no room

Let your heart be filled with so much love,

That resentment has no space to fill even if it tried to claim a spot

Let your heart be owned by love

In the silence, He will meet you

In the loudness of your mind, He will meet you

In any state of being,

He will meet you

If I only knew the Lord during the good, where would be my hope?

We could only know that the Lord is good

If, at times, He was the only good we could find

It is fulfilling

To discover that true goodness is found in Him

And that the fleeting happiness found in this life from time to time

Cannot even compare to the joy that He is at all times

Even in your silence,

He hears the cry of your heart

I think back to Him

When my life looks like a dead end,

I think back to Him

I think back to Him and remember that what seemed
like the end

Was only the beginning

I think back to Him and know that a way is being
made

A way is being made

By the One who left an empty tomb

In place of a grave

A way is being made

By the One who created a new beginning

Where the end seemed inevitable

It is in Him that I live

So when my life looks like a dead end,

I think back to Him

The end of His life

Marks the beginning of mine

Praise Jesus

For His bittersweet sacrifice

The spiral feels endless.

Around and around, I go

Into the familiar pit of infinite despair

That I seem to keep finding myself in

Then I hear Your voice.

Even the loudest of shouts

Cannot compare to the power of Your sweet whisper

Somehow, Your whisper is louder than them all

The sweetness of Your voice brings silence to my
mind

I rest as you untangle the spiral,

As you gather and make beauty

Out of what I thought was a mess,

I rest as all the noise dies down

And Your sweet whisper

Is all that remains

I rest knowing that there is an end to the spiral

That the pit won't be familiar forever

That it will soon become a distant memory

So, as I fight to make this pit an unfamiliar place,

I know You fight with and for me

When the noise takes over,

I cry out to You

And know that You will come to my rescue

When the noise takes over,

I know my soul will recognize that sweet whisper of
Yours

As Your embrace

Becomes my familiar place

Sometimes, the very things you cling to for comfort

Are the chains that are holding you back

Oftentimes, the places that are most comfortable

Are the darkest

Just because you do not know what the light feels like

Does not mean that the darkness is better

Though change can be scary

And the idea of the unknown can be uncomfortable

Don't sacrifice your freedom

For the familiarity of oppression

Don't resist being rescued

Your life is not meant to be a sentence

And you were not made to be a prisoner

Your soul was made for freedom

And freedom you will find

In His presence

Your life is meant to be far more

Than just a feeling of hopelessness

Your days are meant to be filled with far more

Than just the struggle to make it through

Life is meant to be lived and enjoyed

You are not meant to be consumed with the longing
of escape with every passing day

And with desperation for an end as each second goes
by

Life is not meant to be a fight to stay alive

Nor is it meant to feel like a punishment

You are meant to live

Not struggle to survive

Recovery is possible

Recovery is worth it

You are worth it

You are not undeserving of a better life

The largest crowds have the least room

I long for a place to belong

I search and seek for any empty spot that I can fill

I look for a place to belong in the crowd

In any crowd

But I am a misfit in them all

Unwanted and just as alone as I was in my own
solitude,

It is as if my presence makes no difference

Unnoticed and invisible, I walk through, and they
walk right through me

Just as I am giving up on my search for a spot

As I am returning to my hibernation

Dreading the reality of solitude once again

I see You

Your cloak is familiar

They were all moving so fast

But Your cloak

It was there

Still as ever

Were You waiting for me in those crowds?

Did You come just to find me and bring me home?

I remember yearning for someone's gaze

And yet I never realized that Yours was always upon me

I look in Your eyes

And in that sweet gaze of Yours, I know that I have always been seen

I have always been wanted

I have always been noticed

You have a spot just for me

That no one else can fill

I am not just someone else

And to You, I never was

The largest crowds have the least room

But that no longer scares me

As I realize I was never meant to be a part of them in

the first place

Oh, how I long to be in a constant state of gratitude

To live a life in response to the grace of God

To trust,

To recognize,

That my hope is not limited to my circumstances

But in His promises for me

Praise God

For my hope is not confined to the limits of this life

Praise God

For the gift of living in the fullness of life

In a world that is full of death

Don't let your lack of lament

Become a wall between you and the Lord

For He came down from His throne

And clothed Himself in humaneness

He is no stranger to sorrow

From the heavens to all the people of the earth, His compassion flows

From His heart to yours, it is an unending stream

Let yourself feel

For He placed in us a heart made of flesh so that it could be used

Used to love

Used to forgive

Used to feel

He made us to be a reflection of Him

Human with a heart

What a beautiful gift

Underneath it all,

There is a heart of flesh

Words have weight to the heart that is softened

For a hardened heart has no flow

No words pass through

And empty words are all that it can produce

But the softened heart

Allows itself to feel the weight of the words

And knows just how much they truly mean

Be open to the truth

Be open to love

Let not your heart become a hardened shell

When the truth is that underneath it all,

A heart of flesh is made to be soft

The more you hold on to it,

The more of yourself you lose

Let go of the things that are robbing you of yourself

And cling to Him

Your comfort zone is not meant to be made into your home

Don't let the comfort of familiarity

Keep you from the beauty of all the new to come

If where I am is in Your presence,

Then I am right where I am meant to be

Even in the valley of death, there is life

As I dwell in You,

I know that the flowers will bloom wherever I go

For with Your presence comes life

Even in the valley of death, the flowers will bloom

Where Your presence is, there I long to be

For the external does not determine the state of my soul

But it is the One who holds it in His very hands

That determines my place of rest

If He has given you the heart for it,

He will give you the strength to do it

His presence goes with you wherever you go

Don't search for hope and meaning in things that are fleeting

For they will fall through your hands like sand

Why struggle to hold on to the meaningless,

When meaning is being freely offered to you?

Why struggle to keep that fistful of sand in your hand,

When the Giver of all the eternal and everlasting holds all you will ever need in His?

Why settle for a life that leaves you aching for the end,

When the beginning of new life is provided in Him?

Why let your soul settle

for anything less than what it was meant for?

The One who was able to bear all of my brokenness

on His back

Is also able to make me whole

He took it all on

So that He could put an end to it

He is capable

He is able

There is no brokenness too great

No heart He cannot make whole

For on that cross, He thought of you

How He longs to redeem you

There is no cry

That is too far

No whisper

That is too quiet

For His ears to hear

There is no embodiment of love

That is more pure and true

Than the Lover of your soul

You were made for His presence.

His eyes are not closed

You are seen

His ears are not shut

You are heard

His back is not turned

You are wanted

His love pursues you

His arms long to embrace you

Why do you run?

He shapes us and molds us into who He created us to

be

Lord,

May my actions reflect the depths of Your
heart

Here I am

Making myself an offering

And giving myself away

Piece by piece, I fade away

Left with nothing but emptiness,

A face in the mirror that I don't recognize,

And the question that never seems to cease

Who am I?

But with You Jesus,

This is a love I've never known before

A love I've never experienced before

Your presence pours into me

And I am whole

So here I am

Making myself an offering

And giving myself away to You

Piece by piece, you put me back together

The more of myself I give to You

The more of myself I find

The more of my heart You inhabit

The more I come to life

You multiply all that I give to you

You grow fruit out of the parts of me that I thought
were dead

Your love reaches and fills the places in my heart

That I thought would be barren forever

In this world, you are not receiving,

You are being taken from

You are not being filled,

You are being emptied

You are not finding yourself,

You are losing yourself

In a world where emptiness is familiar and typical

Give yourself to Jesus to be filled,

For the only One who can fulfill the soul

Is the One who made it

In a world where all you do is give your heart away
to people who are not capable of filling it

Give your heart to Jesus,

For the only One who is able to fill it

Is the One who formed it

In the midst of repentance

Do not forget to look up to the cross

To see the redemption you have been given

Do not continue to bow your head low in shame

Look up and receive

For condemnation is a long-lasting lie that keeps you

from where you were always meant to be;

In His presence

If you're searching for a reason and have not found one anywhere,

He wants to be yours

The thief comes only to steal and, kill and destroy;

I have come that they may have life, and have it to the full.

John 10:10

Made in the USA
Las Vegas, NV
17 January 2025

16551050R00075